"THE EARTH IS FLAT"
•••••• AND OTHER ••••••
GREAT MISTAKES

LAURENCE PRINGLE is the highly respected author of over forty books for young people on biological and environmental subjects. He lives in West Nyack, New York.

STEVE MILLER's cartoons have appeared in *The New York Times, The Washington Post,* and *Time* magazine. He has also written and illustrated graphic stories for such prominent magazines as *Esquire, Playboy,* and *National Lampoon.* Mr. Miller lives and works in New York City.

"THE EARTH IS FLAT"
·········· AND OTHER ··········
GREAT MISTAKES

LAURENCE PRINGLE

Illustrated by Steve Miller

AN AVON **C** CAMELOT BOOK

Page 1 quotation from Russell Baker copyright © 1982 by *The New York Times Company*. Reprinted by permission.

AVON BOOKS
A division of
The Hearst Corporation
1350 Avenue of the Americas
New York, New York 10019

Text copyright © 1983 by Laurence Pringle
Illustrations copyright © 1983 by Steven B. Miller
Published by arrangement with William Morrow and Company, Inc.
Library of Congress Catalog Card Number: 83-7966
ISBN: 0-380-72319-0
RL: 6.0

The William Morrow and Company edition contains the following Library of Congress Cataloging in Publication Data:

Pringle, Laurence P.
  "The earth is flat"—and other great mistakes.
Includes index. Summary: Examines a variety of blunders and mistakes throughout history, some funny and some tragic, and causes for these errors.
1. Errors—Juvenile literature.   [1. History—Errors, inventions, etc.]
I. Miller, Steve B., ill.   II. Title.
AZ999.P74   1983   001.9'6   83-9766

First Avon Camelot Printing: June 1995

CAMELOT TRADEMARK REG. U.S. PAT. OFF. AND IN OTHER COUNTRIES, MARCA REGISTRADA, HECHO EN U.S.A.

Printed in the U.S.A.

OPM 10 9 8 7 6 5 4 3 2 1

*Dedicated to Lazer Goldberg,
whose wisdom about human error
inspired this book.*

Contents

For Humans Only

"To err is human," wrote Alexander Pope in the eighteenth century. In 1982 humorist Russell Baker expressed the same idea in more specific terms: "I make the average number of mistakes. Maybe 150 or so on a busy day. Most of them aren't terribly serious. Putting too much sugar in the coffee cup. Picking up the telephone and dialing the number of the telephone I've just picked up. Spelling 'harass' with two r's."

Yes, humans make mistakes. They goof, mess up, blunder. They miss, and also mishear, misinterpret, misjudge, mislay, misname, misread, misspeak, misspell, and misunderstand.

Presidents, auto mechanics, students, and authors make mistakes. Everyone does. In fact, making mistakes is so ordinary, so basically human, you may wonder why this book was written. True, most human errors aren't worth noting, but some are extraordinary. They affect many people. They may change the course of history. Some mistakes have had surprisingly good effects, while other blunders have cost billions of dollars and thousands of lives.

This book explores some common causes of human error. Sometimes the cause of a mistake is clear, other times there may be a combination of reasons or several possible explanations. Sometimes the cause is unknown. For example, pyschologists do not understand why certain people misspeak in strange ways. One such person, the English clergyman William Spooner, became famous for saying things like "the queer old dean" when he meant to say "the dear old queen." During a wedding ceremony he said, "It is kisstomary to cuss the bride." Today these mysterious, funny slips of the tongue are called spoonerisms.

This book includes funny blunders as well as tragic ones, great and not-so-great mistakes. Each reveals something about human behavior, and shows some of our best and some of our worst characteristics.

1

On the Frontier

It is easy to make mistakes when you are uninformed, or are working with poor or improper tools. We tend to forget this when we read about the errors of scholars and scientists who lived centuries ago. "Boy, were they stupid!"

So it seems now, but they lived in times of great ignorance. The frontier of knowledge—at the border between the known and unknown—was then in a different place. Moreover, people did not know *how* to go about investigating the world. Too often, they interpreted the unknown in light of what was known —and that was very little. People knew, for example, that they felt jolts and bumps when they rode on a moving wagon. Since they felt none while standing on the ground, they "knew", therefore, that the planet Earth was not moving.

Good minds did try to learn about their world. But the search for truth is always accompanied by errors. Outstanding thinkers were often wrong; they were misleaders as well as leaders.

The most ancient mistakes described on the following pages aren't likely to be repeated. We've learned much about the world over the centuries, and we'll never be that ignorant again. Today's leading thinkers make errors on a new frontier.

Each person also has his or her own frontier of knowledge. Wherever it is, and whether you are learning to drive a car or to speak a new language, you will make some mistakes. It's only human.

THE EARTH IS FLAT

The ancient Babylonians believed that the Earth was flat. In about the eighth century B.C. they described the Earth as a circular plate, supported by four elephants standing on the shell of a sea turtle.

Historians are puzzled by these notions, since a person standing on the shore of an ocean or large lake can watch a departing ship gradually vanish over the horizon—evidence of the Earth's curved surface. They also wonder about the Babylonians' mistaken belief, since these people were active in astronomy and made observations that later led others to conclude that the Earth is a sphere. In any event, the Greek scholar Pythagoras declared in the sixth century B.C. that the Earth was spherical—a fact that has since been confirmed by abundant evidence.

Nevertheless, some people *still* believe the Earth is flat. Their claims are based on their literal interpretation of the Bible, which, for example, refers to "the four corners of the Earth." They belong to the Flat Earth Society, and reject all findings of modern astronomy and space exploration.

EARLY REMEDIES

For a long time, the causes of human illnesses were poorly understood, and this led to some treatments that seem strange today. For example, a person with a fever might have been given turtle soup or snails to eat, or the longest tooth of a fish to wear. The notion was that such "cold," slow-moving creatures would help reduce fever. Trouble with tooth decay? Eat a mouse, or inhale the smoke of burning onion seeds.

Above all, people were warned to avoid breathing night air, and they did so by sealing their bedroom windows and by wearing a scarf over their mouths when they went outdoors at night. In some areas there *was* danger in the night air. People could catch the disease malaria, a word formed from *mala aria* — Italian for "bad air." This bad air was the air around marshes and swamps, places where mosquitoes thrived. Certain kinds of mosquitoes transmitted malaria, while people mistakenly blamed the night air.

DRY WIT

Feeling dull and slow-witted? The ancient Greek philosopher Diogenes had an explanation: too much liquid in the air within your body. According to his idea, humans were smarter than lowly animals because, standing taller, they breathed drier air. A person who acted silly after drinking too much alcohol obviously had rather wet air inside. And little children had short attention spans because air was easily expelled from their small bodies, leaving water inside. They were "overmoist."

This notion was rejected by a later Greek scholar, Theophrastus. If Diogenes was correct, Theophrastus pointed out, then people's intelligence would vary as they traveled through different climates. And the birds of the air would be the most intelligent beings of all.

OFFICIAL NONSENSE

Pliny the Elder, a Roman administrator and writer who lived in the first century A.D., collected all sorts of information about nature, medicine, agriculture, and life in general. He published these thousands of "facts" in a huge book, actually the first encyclopedia, called *Natural History.* The book was popular throughout the Middle Ages and was a basic reference book for fifteen hundred years. But it did nothing to change the ignorance and superstitions prevalent in those times.

Pliny mixed together accurate observations with unsupported claims and fables. He wrote of women giving birth to elephants, and of cats driving people "into madness" by simply licking the humans' skin with their rough tongues. He claimed that mouse droppings, rubbed into one's head, caused hair to grow on a bald spot, and that earwax healed wounds caused by poisonous scorpions and serpents. Pliny's *Natural History* has been called "the greatest single repository of misinformation known to man."

Competition for this honor comes from the works of Galen, a Roman physician of the second century A.D. He studied medicine and human anatomy. Doctors today still use the names that Galen gave to certain muscles. Some of his ideas were partly correct, but most were not. He was a forceful speaker and a prolific writer, however, and his books seemed to have an answer for everything. They were endorsed by the most powerful authority of those times, the Roman Catholic Church.

Galen's written words were the basic reference in medicine for the next fourteen centuries. These were mostly times when both fact and fallacy were blindly accepted. As a result there was little progress in understanding how the human body worked and how to treat disease. The practice of medicine was dominated by strange beliefs and useless treatments.

Then, in the sixteenth century, Andreas Vesalius, a doctor at the University of Padua in Italy, published a book on the structure of the human body. In a modest way, Vesalius dared to question Galen. From actual dissection, for example, he had learned that men and women had the same number of ribs. This was disturbing news to many people. Since the Scriptures taught that Eve had been created from Adam's rib, men were supposed to have one less rib than

women. Vesalius's finding was resented, but he was allowed to go on teaching. He influenced his students, who began to observe and investigate for themselves. After centuries of enforced ignorance, there was change on the frontier of knowledge in medicine.

SMALL WORLD

A combination of mistaken ideas about geography played a crucial role in the first voyage of Christopher Columbus. One mistake involved the size of the Earth. Since the time of ancient Greece, scholars had believed that the Earth was a sphere. And if this was true, it would be possible to sail west from Europe and eventually come to Asia. But could anyone sail that far without running out of food and water? How big around was the Earth?

In about 240 B.C., Eratosthenes, a Greek geographer, correctly estimated that the Earth's circumference was 24,000 miles. Later Greek geographers, however, estimated that the Earth was only about 17,400 miles around.

Another misconception was Marco Polo's information about Asia's location, which placed it farther east than it really is. Together, these two mistakes indicated that no more than 2,880 miles lay between western Europe and Asia. This was less than one-fifth the real distance. It was a big error but a lucky one because it encouraged Columbus to believe that he could sail west and find Asia.

He convinced Spain's rulers to finance the voyage, and set out in 1492. Fortunately for Columbus and his crew, the continents of North and South America lay partway in the vast distance between Europe and Asia. On October 12, 1492, Columbus's three ships reached islands he mistakenly thought were the Indies—as Asia was then called—so he named the natives "Indians." He believed he was near Japan.

Columbus explored the region on three later voyages, and landed on what we now call Trinidad and Honduras. Other explorers had begun to claim that new continents had been found, but when Columbus died in 1506, he still believed that he had sailed around the world to Asia.

THE CANALS OF MARS

In 1877 an Italian astronomer named Giovanni Schiaparelli was observing the planet Mars through a telescope. The atmospheric conditions were excellent for clear viewing, and Schiaparelli saw what appeared to be long, narrow marks on the surface of Mars. He called them *canali,* the Italian word that means "channels"; but in English his discovery was mistakenly translated as "canals."

This caused great excitement. A channel can be a natural feature of a landscape; but canals, on Earth at least, are made only by humans. Could this be evidence of life on Mars?

Yes, said noted astronomer Percival Lowell, director of the observatory at Flagstaff, Arizona. He too saw networks of canals on Mars, and drew about five hundred of them. Lowell believed that Martians had built the canals in order to bring water from polar ice caps to other parts of their planet.

Other astronomers also believed that they saw the faint markings on Mars. Some did not. Martian canals were still a matter of controversy when Lowell died in 1916.

Eventually, as telescopes improved in quality, fewer astronomers reported seeing canals. And clear photographs taken from space satellites and from the actual surface of Mars show neither canals nor any surface features that could have been mistaken for them. Schiaparelli's "channels" and Lowell's "canals" were apparently some sort of optical illusion, made possible by the poor-quality telescopes of their times.

KUDZU

We now know that almost any plant or animal brought from one continent to another means potential trouble. In its new environment, the alien organism may become a serious pest because natural enemies, which normally keep its numbers in check, are usually absent. Because people were ignorant about ecology, however, for many years there were no laws forbidding the importation of foreign organisms to North America. As a result, we have well-established populations of such animals as starlings, English sparrows, and Japanese beetles. Among plants, the alien invaders include water chestnuts, water hyacinths, and kudzu—a fast-growing vine that was imported from Japan in 1876.

Kudzu is a particularly glaring case of human folly because this nuisance was once promoted and deliberately planted throughout the South. It was used first as an ornamental vine, providing shade around porches. Someone then noticed that livestock ate kudzu; and investigation also showed that the plant helped restore nitrogen to the soil. By the 1930s, government agencies were helping people plant kudzu all over the southern states.

By the 1950s, however, farmers had discovered that kudzu was not such great cattle forage after all, and the vine was running wild over the land. Kudzu blanketed fields and abandoned buildings. It climbed trees and utility poles. The thick foliage cast so much shade that trees died.

Even today, utility companies spend millions of dollars each year spraying herbicides to clear kudzu from poles and towers; and government agencies give advice on how to get rid of kudzu rather than on how to plant it.

Recently, filmmakers produced a movie called

Kurse of the Kudzu Kreature. It was a spoof of monster movies, but to many southerners the title suggested that it was a realistic documentary.

DANGER ON THE FRONTIER

A lack of information can sometimes have deadly consequences, as in the case of Marie Curie. She was a Polish-born French chemist, who, with her husband, Pierre, investigated chemical elements to learn about the newly discovered phenomenon called radioactivity. After Pierre died in a traffic accident in 1906, Marie Curie continued research on such radioactive substances as polonium and radium. She also studied X rays and their application in medicine. Marie Curie is the only person to win two Nobel Prizes for achievements in science, one in physics and one in chemistry.

Eventually, both X rays and radioactive substances were found to have harmful effects—knowledge that came too late to help people who had been routinely exposed to large doses of radiation. In 1934 Marie Curie died of leukemia, cancer of the blood, which was caused by excessive exposure to radiation.

ROMAN HOLIDAY

Fortunately, most mistakes do not cause much harm. For example, in 1977 Nicholas Scotti of San Francisco decided to visit relatives in Italy. Although a United States citizen, he read and spoke little English. When his airplane stopped briefly in New York, Mr. Scotti got out, believing that he had arrived in Rome.

He spent two days wandering around the city, trying to track down his relatives. He noticed many signs written in English and heard people speaking English with American accents, but assumed they were tourists and that the signs were for their benefit. Once he asked a policeman the way to the bus depot. The policeman, who came originally from Naples, replied in fluent Italian.

Eventually, Mr. Scotti's mistake was discovered. He was put on an airplane back to San Francisco, still half-believing that he had been in Rome.

2
Plan Ahead

"The best laid schemes of mice and men often go awry," wrote the Scottish poet Robert Burns. As it turns out, such plans are actually not so well laid because they are vulnerable to little oversights, carelessness, unforeseen events, inadequate preparations —or a combination of such factors. Some of the examples on the following pages represent costly projects that went awry despite the best efforts of many highly skilled workers. Is it any wonder, then, that ordinary folks sometimes find that their plans don't work out?

TILT

In the year 1174, work began on a bell tower for the cathedral in Pisa, Italy. It was designed to stand about 180 feet high. As its graceful marble form rose higher and higher, however, the builders discovered a terrible mistake. The ten-foot-thick foundation beneath the tower was not strong enough, and the whole tower began to tilt to one side.

Work was halted. The bell tower stood unfinished for more than a century as new architects proposed ways to make the tower appear to tilt less, and some remedies were eventually tried. The building was finally completed in 1350, but its heavy marble base, with walls thirteen feet thick, continued to settle. By the early 1980s, the top of the tower was tilted about seventeen feet from vertical, and each year it leans a fraction of an inch more.

Many architects and engineers have devised plans to halt the tilt of the tower. No attempted remedy has worked. In fact, the tower leaned even farther after nine hundred tons of concrete were pumped into holes dug under its low side in 1934. Today, the people of Pisa do not want their tower straightened. They just hope that their leaning tower—a great tourist attraction—will not become the "fallen tower of Pisa."

WANDERING GYPSIES

A French artist and entomologist, Leopold Trouvelot, imported some caterpillars to eastern Massachusetts in 1869. The caterpillars were fond of leaves from oaks, common trees in the eastern United States. Trouvelot planned to make a fortune for himself by crossbreeding the adult forms of these caterpillars, called gypsy moths, with the moths of silkworms. The result, he hoped, would be a silk-producing caterpillar that thrived on oak leaves.

The crossbreeding didn't work, however, and one

day a gust of wind toppled a caterpillar cage in Trouvelot's house. Gypsy-moth caterpillars crawled out the open window, escaped, and survived. The moths spread slowly at first and at one point the state of Massachusetts came very close to wiping out the pests. By 1950, however, gypsy moths could be found in all the New England states and eastern New York. They have since spread as far as Virginia and Maryland. New moth populations have become established in Indiana, Minnesota, and California—probably the result of egg masses laid on vehicles that were driven from the Northeast to other regions.

Gypsy moth numbers rise and fall over a span of five or six years. During the 1981 population peak, caterpillars reportedly stripped leaves from thirteen million acres of trees and caused some weak trees to die.

However, the caterpillars are mostly a nuisance, especially when they chew all the leaves from shade trees around homes and their frass, or droppings, rain down on passersby. Some people seek to control them with insect poisons, while others believe it is cheaper and safer to let the moth numbers decline naturally and to encourage the natural checks on their population, which include diseases, parasitic flies and wasps, and such predators as mice and birds.

All things considered, everyone agrees that they would have been better off if the moths had been kept out of this country, and if the wind hadn't blown over that cage.

TUNNEL VISION

In 1975 convicts at Saltillo Prison in northern Mexico spent several months digging a secret tunnel, carefully planned to reach beyond the prison's walls. The plan worked, but only up to a point. The tunnel *did* lead out of the prison, as seventy-five convicts discovered when they emerged in a nearby court-room. They were quickly recaptured.

GALLOPING GERTIE

July 1, 1940, marked the opening of the Tacoma Narrows Bridge across Puget Sound in Washington. Costing $6.5 million, it was 2,800 feet long—the world's third largest suspension bridge at that time. During construction, workers noticed that the deck supporting the bridge highway moved a great deal in the wind. In fact, some workers became ill as the surface undulated beneath their feet. Once the bridge opened, however, this feature became a great attraction. Traffic was much heavier than anticipated because people drove across the bridge just for fun. The bridge became known as Galloping Gertie.

The fun stopped in November 1940 on a day of

steady 42-miles-per-hour winds. The bridge deck undulated more and more violently. The last few rides across Galloping Gertie were the best, if the people in the cars enjoyed roller coasters at amusement parks. One car was abandoned in the middle of the span, and the bridge was closed to traffic. Then, still swinging wildly in the wind, the deck began to come apart and fall into the water below. Soon the bridge cables were suspending nothing—Galloping Gertie was gone.

Investigation showed that the deck had been built too much like a solid wall, or an airplane wing, so that it caught the wind. Since the death of Galloping Gertie, models of proposed suspension bridges are made and tested in wind tunnels before the bridge actually is built.

MUDDLING ALONG WITH QWERT

When C. L. Sholes was inventing a typewriting machine in the early 1870s, he found that the machine jammed if he typed too fast. So he deliberately arranged the positions of the letters in a way that forced typists to work more slowly. Nevertheless, Sholes's typewriter design was still a great improvement over earlier models, and so it was soon in use all over the world.

Today, even though typewriters have been im-

proved in many ways, nearly all of them have keyboards like the one Sholes devised in 1872. The letter arrangement is called QWERT, after the five left-hand keys in the top letter row. You can see QWERT keyboards on computer consoles, as well as on typewriters. Unfortunately, the QWERT arrangement slows typing, encourages errors, and causes greater fatigue than another arrangement, devised by August Dvorak in 1930, which has proved in several tests to be much faster and more accurate than QWERT. However, millions of people have learned the QWERT keyboard; and, in fact, it is being taught to students in schools right now. So it seems that we will continue to live with this nineteenth-century mistake.

LITTLE THINGS MEAN A LOT

In 1962 an Atlas-Agena rocket was launched from Florida. It was supposed to carry the Mariner 1 satellite into space for its journey to Venus. But the rocket veered off course. Ground controllers signaled the rocket to self-destruct, and it exploded. An investigation showed that the rocket flew erratically because of one flaw in its computer program. Someone had left out a minus sign, and this little missing detail cost taxpayers $18.5 million.

This is an apt illustration of a modern saying: "To err is human; to really foul things up takes a computer."

PLYWOOD PALACE

Designed by a world-famous architectural firm, the John Hancock Tower is Boston's tallest building. After years of planning, construction of this sixty-story, glass-sheathed building began in 1968. It was completed in 1972 at a cost of $150 million—but wasn't occupied until 1976. The reason for this delay: breaking and falling glass.

The tower has 10,344 large panes of glass, and windows started breaking even before it was complete. Then, in January 1973, a storm with 75-miles-per-hour winds struck Boston. Sixty-five panes shattered and showered the sidewalks below. Glass fragments, raining down the building's west side, damaged hundreds of other windows. About a quarter of the tower's surface was boarded up while studies went on. The building became known as the Plywood Palace.

At first the glass was thought to be defective, and its maker was sued for damages. However, tests showed that at least part of the problem was the building itself. All skyscrapers sway a bit in the wind, but this tower's design produced strong movement that put an extra strain on its windows.

This motion has since been reduced by massive inner weights, and all the glass has been replaced with stronger panes. Several years later than planned, the former Plywood Palace became the dominant glass office tower of the Boston skyline.

THE UTILITY'S FAULT

For years, Pacific Gas & Electric Company, the nation's largest utility, sought to build and operate nuclear power plants at Diablo Canyon, on the California coast. A site far from any known earthquake fault was chosen, but the utility neglected to look under the sea. In 1972 it learned that the Hosgri fault lay only 2½ miles offshore.

The Nuclear Regulatory Commission, which is responsible for the safety of nuclear power plants, was not told about this discovery for a year. And once it was told, the commission allowed construction to go

on while geologists investigated the fault. One nuclear plant was three-quarters complete before geologists concluded that a very strong earthquake might some-day occur there.

Antinuclear groups sought to halt construction. Failing that, they tried to keep the Diablo Canyon plants from operating. But the Nuclear Regulatory Commission gave permission for the completed plant to operate, beginning at low power. In September 1981 uranium fuel was about to be loaded. Everything was set to begin. Then utility workers discovered that the wrong plans had been used to build parts of the plant. Blueprints for the two adjoining plants had been switched. The second plant, nearly complete, was also built incorrectly. Hundreds of changes, involving supports for pipes, emergency cooling fans, and other vital equipment, were required.

A member of the commission said that the utility's mistake was like "a student copying down the wrong homework assignment. No matter how brilliant the work from then on, he's just not going to get the right answers."

3
Misjudgments

People must make judgments every day: whether to swing at a pitch, whether a melon is ripe enough to eat, whether a new drug is safe and effective and can be sold to the public. With enough knowledge and experience about some matters, a person can judge accurately much of the time—there *are* ways to tell whether a melon is ripe. There are also plenty of opportunities to be mistaken. Every day, individuals, companies, and government leaders decide whether to take certain actions. Sometimes the results are instantaneous: you swing the bat and hit or miss the ball. In other situations the results may not be known for years or decades, or people may never agree whether a choice was wise or foolish.

THE CLOUDY CRYSTAL BALL

Predictions are judgments about the future. Authorities in various fields have had some success in predicting future developments. In the past few years, for example, geologists have successfully predicted a few earthquakes. Overall, though, experts through the ages have made some extraordinary misjudgments:

"Any general system of conveying passengers—at a velocity exceeding 10 miles per hour, or thereabouts —is extremely improbable."

—Thomas Tredgold,
British railroad designer,
1835

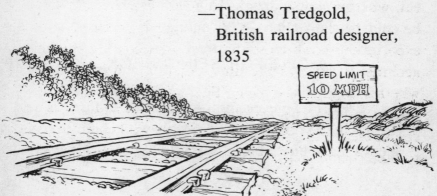

"That is the biggest fool thing we have ever done . . . The bomb will never go off, and I speak as an expert in explosives."

—Admiral William Leahy,
U.S. Navy officer, speaking
to President Harry Truman
about the atomic bomb in 1945

"Landing and moving around the moon offers so many serious problems for human beings that it may take science another 200 years to lick them."

—*Science Digest,* 1948

"I confess that in 1901, I said to my brother Orville that man would not fly for 50 years . . . Ever since, I have distrusted myself and avoided all predictions."

—Wilbur Wright, speaking in 1908,
after his brother flew successfully
in 1903

A GIFT FOR BEING WRONG

A great and never-ending series of failures is recorded in the predictions of people who claim to have special "psychic" ability to foretell events. Their predictions are often printed in tabloid periodicals sold at supermarkets and newsstands. When 364 predictions from ten psychics that had been printed in the *National Enquirer* during 1976–79 were investigated, 98.9 percent were found to be wrong.

Another investigation into the accuracy of psychics showed that only about 16 percent of their predictions were accurate. Their limited success came mostly from such vaguely worded forecasts as "there will be trouble in the Middle East." This, unfortunately, seems to be a safe prediction in almost any year. Another safe prediction: So-called psychics will almost always be wrong.

THE DUMB KID

Married in 1876, Hermann and Pauline Einstein had a baby boy in 1879. They named him Albert. As he grew up in Munich, Germany, his parents became increasingly worried about him. He did not talk until he was three. When he grew older, he sometimes replied to a question only after much thought. The Einsteins feared that Albert's intelligence was below normal. Teachers suspected that he was dull-witted too. When asked what profession Albert should prepare for, his school headmaster offered this judgment: "It doesn't matter; he'll never make a success of anything."

Albert did show skill in mathematics, but he rebelled against the strict discipline of German schools. He thought of the teachers as sergeants and lieutenants. His disrespect for some teachers was quite clear, apparently, because he was expelled from high school without a diploma.

This shaky start did not prevent Albert Einstein from making revolutionary discoveries about matter and energy. Although he died in 1955, his name continues to stand as a synonym for great intelligence, for genius. Even today, people often call a bright child "a little Einstein," unaware that young Albert was mistakenly considered to be a dumb kid.

LEMON

The Ford Motor Company had high hopes for the Edsel, a car introduced to buyers in 1957. It was more than a new car; it was to be the beginning of an entire new division of the automaking company. The Edsel was Ford's first attempt to break into the upper-middle-class market. With it the company hoped to compete with the Buicks, Pontiacs, and Oldsmobiles of General Motors. The car had been carefully planned for several years, and was introduced with great fanfare.

But the years 1957–58 were a time of recession, and expensive cars were not selling well. Furthermore, the Edsel's looks, especially its distinctive front end, became a source of jokes. Its vertical grill had been designed to look somewhat like a Rolls Royce. Instead, it reminded people of a horse collar, or of someone pursing has his or her lips in response to a bitter lemon taste.

After one year of production, Ford halted its great Edsel venture forever.

TELL ME WHY

In the early 1960s, a rock-and-roll band from Liverpool, England, tried to get their songs recorded. Several companies turned them down. "We don't like their sound," said a spokesman for Decca Records. "Groups of guitars are on the way out."

Eventually, EMI Records decided to take a chance on the Beatles.

EYEWITNESS

In 1980 a priest was arrested for committing several robberies. The evidence against him was strong. Several witnesses identified him positively, and he seemed headed for conviction and prison. Then another man was caught committing a robbery, and he confessed to the crimes the priest had "committed." The priest was lucky. Other innocent people have spent years in prison, largely because of the misjudgments of eyewitnesses.

The words "I saw it with my own eyes" have power. Judges and juries tend to put great faith in such testimony. Yet research shows that eyewitnesses "see" selectively and often inaccurately. Men and women recall different details. If ten people witness an event, each one describes it differently. And questions asked by a policeman or lawyer can affect what a witness recalls.

For example, consider these two questions: "Did you see a broken headlight?" and "Did you see the broken headlight?" When different groups of students were shown a film of an automobile accident, then questioned about what they had witnessed, more of the students who were asked about *the* broken headlight recalled such a headlight than those who were asked about *a* broken headlight. (The film showed no broken headlight.)

Eyewitness testimony has also proved to be unreliable in matters other than crime. Each year when the planet Venus is brightest in the night sky, thousands of people imagine it to be a flying saucer or other such unidentified flying object. People tend to see what they want to see.

WAR OF THE WORLDS

In 1938 Orson Welles directed a series of weekly dramatic programs on the CBS radio network. For the broadcast on Halloween eve, Welles had a writer prepare a script that was adapted from H.G. Wells's science-fiction novel, *War of the Worlds*—a story of hostile forces from Mars invading the Earth. Welles and his staff felt that the script was rather silly. He considered substituting another story but did not, and radio waves carried the hour-long dramatization of *War of the Worlds* out into the late October night.

As the drama began, it seemed to be a program of dance music performed by a hotel orchestra. The music was interrupted by a news bulletin about disturbances detected on Mars. The music

"IT'S OKAY, MARTHA — IT'S JUST TRICK-OR-TREATERS."

resumed, then was interrupted again, and again. Gradually, the whole show was taken over with "on-the-spot" reports—of spaceships armed with poison gas landing in New Jersey, of New York City destroyed.

Four times during the program, radio audiences were told that they were listening to a dramatization; and Welles himself announced at its end, "That was no Martian . . . it's Halloween." Nevertheless, thousands of people from coast to coast took the broadcast seriously. They ran to warn neighbors, fled in cars, overloaded telephone systems, prayed, and panicked. Fortunately, no one died of a heart attack, though many people were treated for shock. The script that Orson Welles almost discarded had caused mass hysteria, and was unintentionally one of the most successful hoaxes of all time.

SUPERBOMB

In 1949 the Soviet Union exploded its first atomic bomb. This was disturbing news in the United States. Although scientists had predicted that other nations would develop atomic weapons, the actual accomplishment by America's "cold war" enemy was a shock. It marked the end of a period in which the United States had a monopoly on the most powerful weapon then known.

The question was: What should the United States do? Only a few dozen men, including scientists who had developed the first American atomic weapons, studied this matter and advised President Harry S Truman. In the judgment of some of these experts, there was just one correct response: Develop the superbomb. This bomb, also called the H-bomb (for hydrogen), was already under study. Not to build it, they argued, would leave the United States weak and vulnerable to Soviet attack.

Other scientists believed that the superbomb was too big and deadly. They were alarmed about the possible global effects of radioactivity from the explosion of several H-bombs. They believed that the United States would be strong enough with its large stock of improved atomic bombs, even if the Soviets developed the superbomb. This group of experts urged that the United States set an example for the world, by announcing that it was not building the H-bomb, and by urging international control of weapons of mass destruction.

In January 1950, President Truman chose to go ahead with development of the H-bomb. Some scientists who worked on it actually hoped that it would not work, but it did. The first test, in November 1952, yielded about a thousand times more energy than the atomic bomb dropped on Hiroshima, Japan, in 1945. Three years later the Soviet Union exploded its first H-bomb. The arms race accelerated, and continues to this day.

Some people believe that President Truman made the right choice in 1952. Others believe that the United States lost a great opportunity to be the first nation to choose not to build a new means of killing people. Three decades later, people still disagree about whether the right choice was made. This is one of those complex judgments about which people may never agree.

4

Don't Confuse Me with the Facts

The man removed all the toy parts from the carton and began putting them together. An hour later, fussing and fuming, he still didn't have them assembled correctly. As gently as possible, his wife said, "If all else fails, try following directions."

Sometimes, of course, directions are unclear or incomplete, and contribute to failure. But there's also that human urge to plunge ahead, to act, to pursue an idea without much thought, help, or preparation. Sometimes people are so eager for results, or ambitious, or greedy, that they ignore warning signs that failure may lie ahead.

Another equally strong human trait is the resolution *not* to act. Some people cling tightly to ideas or behavior patterns, even though there are signs that change would be wise. They may be greatly tempted to change but feel that the risk of change is greater than the risk of not changing.

Either way, plunging ahead or standing pat, people seem to say, "My mind is made up, don't confuse me with the facts."

THE PAINTED BULLS

In 1875 a Spanish nobleman named Don Marcelino de Sautuola heard of a cave on his estate near a hill called Altamira. Being interested in geology, he visited the cave. Inside he found large bones, which he later learned were from a bison, a wild horse, and an extinct giant stag. Many of the bones were split lengthwise—evidence that humans had once opened them to eat the marrow.

In Paris a few years later, Don Marcelino saw an exhibit of prehistoric arrowheads and stone tools found in French caves. He decided to explore his own

cave further. Sure enough, he found some stone tools.
For several days the nobleman continued to look and
to dig on the cave floor. One day his nine-year-old
daughter, Maria, asked to come with him. Don Marcelino took her along, and eventually she explored
deeper into the cavern as he worked.

Suddenly she shouted, "Papa, Papa! Look! Painted
bulls!" He hurried to her, and followed her gaze to-
ward the ceiling. In the flickering lamplight he saw
colored paintings of a herd of charging, giant bison.
The paintings covered the entire ceiling of an area he
had passed through many times. Don Marcelino had
always been looking down, for objects on the floor.

Maria had looked all around. Together they found many other paintings in the cave. Although they did not know it at the time, they had discovered the first known paintings of humans who lived at least fourteen thousand years ago.

A report of the Altamira cave paintings was published in 1880. But the experts on prehistoric humans had certain set ideas. They did not believe that people who relied on stone tools and who lived in caves could make grand paintings. Apparently, they did not want to look at evidence that might alter their beliefs. The paintings were a hoax, said the experts, and Don Marcelino was considered a fraud.

Several years after his death in 1888, other cave paintings were discovered in France. This opened the experts' eyes to the art of prehistoric people. Their change of mind came too late to correct their injustice to Don Marcelino, but one archaeology professor traveled to Altamira to apologize in person to Maria.

DEAD WRONG

Through the ages military battles have offered many examples of human error. Indeed, entire wars have later been judged to be terrible wastes of resources and human lives. This seems to be true of the tragic conflict that occurred in the American West after the Civil War. Some Indian tribes refused to leave their ancestral lands granted to them by treaties which were later broken by the United States government. In order to advance their careers, ambitious army officers used the Plains as a kind of gaming field, seeking military victories over Indians, including women and children. One of these officers, General George Armstrong Custer, believed that the glory of a victory might lead to his becoming the Democratic candidate for President. At a luncheon in New York City, Custer boasted that his Seventh Cavalry could "whip all of the Indians on the Plains."

In late June 1876, Custer led the Seventh Cavalry south from the Yellowstone River in Montana Territory, planning to drive any Indians from the region. The cavalry's scouts became increasingly worried as they advanced. Somewhere ahead, the Teton Sioux, Northern Cheyennes, and some Arapahos were holding a great annual meeting. As the cavalry drew closer to the big encampment on the Little Bighorn River, scouts found wide areas that had been grazed by thousands of Indian ponies. This and other signs indicated that Custer's men were badly outnumbered. A scout warned Custer, "Get your outfit out of the country as fast as your played-out horses can carry you."

But Custer pressed on. He began a poorly planned

attack, dividing his force of 650 men into three groups. There is speculation that Custer did this to keep other officers from sharing in his victory. Instead, this tactic ensured his defeat. Custer and 224 of his men were wiped out.

PERCHANCE A REVISION OF **TACTICS** MIGHT BE IN ORDER...

"PRACTICALLY UNSINKABLE"

A British journal, *The Shipbuilder,* called the new *Titanic* "practically unsinkable." The hull of the 900-foot-long ocean liner was divided into sixteen separate compartments. Any two of these compartments could be flooded without harm coming to the rest of the ship.

The most luxurious ship afloat, the *Titanic* was the first to have a swimming pool. It was called the "Millionaire's Special" and the "Wonder Ship."

The *Titanic* set out on its first cross-Atlantic voyage in April 1912 with 915 crew members and 1,320 passengers. For the first four days and nights, all went well. Halfway across the North Atlantic, the *Titanic* was right on schedule.

Although the ship's captain had been warned about icebergs in the vicinity, the *Titanic* was under full power near midnight on April 15 when an iceberg loomed ahead. There wasn't enough time to avoid a collision. Crewmen heard a "slight grinding noise" or felt a "slight jar." For a few moments it seemed that the ship had just had a close call. But the iceberg had ripped a 300-foot-long gash in the ship's side. Water flooded five compartments, and the *Titanic* began to sink.

Lifeboats had been provided for only about half the people on board. The number of lifeboats met the safety regulations of the British government, which had not yet changed its rulings to take into account the great size of new ships like the *Titanic*. Loading of the lifeboats was mismanaged, and some were only partly occupied when they pulled away from the ship. In all, 1,522 people drowned or froze to death in the icy waters as the *Titanic* sank two thousand fathoms to the bottom of the North Atlantic.

FEMALE BRAINS

Less than a century ago, women were considered inferior to men in many ways, including in intelligence. This idea was just "common sense" in the nineteenth century.

In 1879, for example, a prominent French scientist by the name of Gustave Le Bon wrote of women: "They represent the most inferior forms of human evolution . . . closer to children and savages than to an adult, civilized man."

Some anthropologists believed that certain inherited, physical characteristics accounted for a person's intelligence, or his or her place in society. Paul Broca, a French surgeon, was a leader in the search for evidence to support this idea. He believed that he had found it in four Parisian hospitals where he personally weighed the brains of several hundred patients who had died. Sure enough, women had smaller brains than men.

That clinched it; here was actual proof, accurate measurements that demonstrated female inferiority. Although Broca died in 1880, his findings lived on, frequently cited by his followers.

But numbers, by themselves, are meaningless. Broca's measurements were accurate, all right, but they proved nothing. First of all, Broca had overlooked some reasons that could account for the differences he found in brain weights. For example, brains shrink as people age, and most of the female patients whose brains Broca measured were much older than the male patients.

More important, it was later learned that intelligence has nothing to do with the size of the brain. Of course, Broca and his supporters cannot be faulted for being ignorant of this fact. Their greatest mistake was their unquestioning acceptance of a commonly held belief—that certain kinds of people were born inferior —and their quest for evidence to support that prejudice.

MAYBE NEXT TIME

An Englishman named Arthur Paul Pedrick obtained patents on 162 of his inventions. They included a bicycle that could cross streams and lakes, a golf ball that could be steered in flight (which, by the rules of the game, would be illegal), and an irrigation scheme that involved sending snowballs from polar regions through a network of giant tubes to deserts.

Not a single one of Pedrick's ideas was ever developed or produced commercially.

FOR SOME THE WAR WENT ON,
AND ON, AND ON

On September 2, 1945, war between Japan and the Allied Forces, including the United States, officially ended. World War II was finally over. Japanese forces were withdrawn from scores of far-flung bases, including many islands in the Pacific.

But in March 1974, a Japanese army lieutenant was found in the jungle of a remote island in the Philippines. In 1945, when letters announcing the war's end had been dropped onto his island from airplanes, he had dismissed them as a trick to make him surrender.

Later that same year, another Japanese soldier gave up his isolated outpost on an Indonesian island. It took several months to convince both men that the war had ended twenty-nine years earlier.

5

Taking a Chance

To make as few errors as possible, do as little as possible. This will greatly reduce your chances of failing, or making mistakes, but it will also lead to a dull life. People seem to thrive when they allow themselves to change, to try new ideas.

There is risk, of course, whenever someone tries something new. Such people are pioneers, whether they are exploring something new in the universe or new in themselves. Pioneers risk feeling embarrassed, being laughed at, or harming their careers or reputations. Some people even risk their lives.

Worrying about errors and failure may make matters worse. A California woman, for example, was so worried about failing her test for a driver's license that she mistook the car's accelerator for its clutch and drove through the wall of the test center. Some students don't do very well on examinations simply because of their anxiety. Fear of making errors or of failing can be a very strong feeling.

Perhaps it will help to recall how much we respect people who have been pioneers, who have dared to take a chance. In sports and in other human endeavors, we admire daring people, even if they fail. Some of our greatest heroes have been wrong at times, or made mistakes, but we don't think less of them for it. They tried, in a courageous or imaginative way, and this is admirable.

DEADLY DOUBTS

If you like to avoid thinking, having doubts, and asking questions, you might have *loved* living during Europe's Dark Ages, which covered all but the last few centuries of the past two thousand years. Astronomy and other sciences were valued only if they reinforced what was already "known." The authority was the Scriptures, as interpreted by the Roman Catholic Church.

It was easier to agree than to doubt and question. The few people who dared to challenge accepted beliefs were often dealt with severely. Giordano Bruno, an Italian philosopher, had his doubts. He doubted that God looked down on the universe, and believed instead that God was everywhere, in all things. He also believed that there might be other inhabited planets in the universe.

Arrested in 1593, Bruno was imprisoned in a dungeon for seven years. Retract those ideas, he was told, or else. He refused and was burned at the stake in the year 1600.

"THE WAY THE HEAVENS GO"

One basic notion accepted as the truth during the Dark Ages was that the Earth was the center of the universe, with other planets and the sun revolving around it. In 1543 a Polish cleric named Nicholas Copernicus published another theory—that the sun was the center of the universe, with the Earth and other planets circling it. It seems that Copernicus deliberately delayed publishing his ideas until he was old and ill. He died in the same year his book was published, and so could not be persecuted. His ideas lived on, although in 1616 the Church put Copernicus's work on a list of forbidden books, where it remained until 1835. Nevertheless, his book was widely read. Though his sun-centered model of the universe was incorrect, Copernicus had started a complete change in people's concept of the universe.

Galileo Galilei was another pioneer who dared to investigate rather than accept the "wisdom" of the times. As the seventeenth century began he was teaching mathematics at the University of Padua in Italy. In 1609 he made a simple telescope. Through it he observed the rough texture of the moon's surface, spots on the sun, and four moons orbiting Jupiter. This last discovery upset those people who believed that there could be only seven objects in the heavens and no more.

Galileo urged other men at his university to look through his telescope, but they declined. Commenting on their refusal, Galileo wrote to a friend: "What would you say of the learned here, who, afflicted with the stubbornness of the ass, steadfastly have refused to cast a glance through the telescope? What shall we make of all this? Shall we laugh, or shall we cry?"

Galileo supported the idea that the Earth revolved around the sun, and before long, he was in big trouble with the Church. Biblical scholars declared that it was foolish and contrary to Scripture to hold that the Earth was moving. Defending himself, Galileo wrote that, "The Bible shows the way to go to heaven, not the way the heavens go." Galileo was admonished to give up this idea; he would be imprisoned if he taught or discussed his views. At first Galileo seemed to comply; but then he wrote a book, published in 1632, which supported Copernicus's ideas. Threatened with torture, Galileo again renounced his views. He was

permitted to live the last few years of his life on his farm.

In 1979, nearly three hundred fifty years later, Pope John Paul II said that Galileo had "suffered at the hands of men and the institutions of the Church." The Vatican has since announced that the Galileo case will be reopened.

Both Galileo and Copernicus had several mistaken ideas. Galileo's explanation of the ocean's tides, for example, was incorrect. But today we remember these men's courage and questioning attitudes, not whether they were always right.

AERONAUTS

As early as 1742, a Frenchman built birdlike wings for himself, flapped off his Paris roof, and broke his leg as he fell onto the deck of a barge. The first manned balloon flights, in France and England, were remarkably free of mishaps, but disaster was inevitable. In 1785 two men attempted to cross the English Channel by hydrogen-filled balloon. It caught fire and the men fell five thousand feet to their deaths.

In 1804, when Count Zambeccari and two assistants took off from Bologna, Italy, their balloon rose so high that they almost froze to death. The balloon

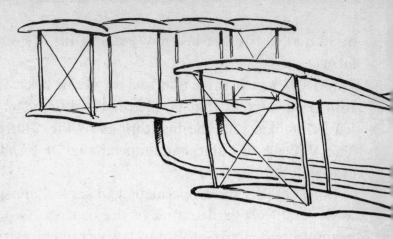

began descending in the dark, but the men didn't have enough light to read a barometer and estimate their height. They heard the roar of waves too late, and the balloon landed in the Adriatic Sea. The men threw ballast and other objects overboard, and the lightened balloon shot upward again—so high that their sea-soaked clothes froze and they could hardly breathe. The balloon came down slowly and fell into the sea again. The men were rescued after dawn. All three suffered from frostbite, and Zambeccari had to have parts of his fingers amputated. Undaunted, the Count continued to go aloft in balloons. When his balloon caught fire at treetop level in 1812, Zambeccari jumped, and died of his injuries.

Nevertheless, other balloonists learned from these mistakes, and from their own errors and successes.

TO FLY

Count Zambeccari's exploits influenced at least one other pioneer of flight. Otto Lilienthal was a German engineer who read of the count's aerial adventures and began experimenting with flying machines. As a youth, he and his brother tried, with some success, to glide by running down a steep hill with wings fastened to their arms. Otto studied bird flight and the structure of bird wings, then designed gliders based on his observations. Near Berlin, he began making glides eight hundred feet or more long, with heights of a hundred feet. He also made progress in learning how to control a glider in flight. Then, in 1896, after more than two thousand successful flights, Otto Lilienthal was testing a new rudder design when his glider went into a nose dive from a height of about fifty feet. He was killed.

Four thousand miles away, in Ohio, the Wright brothers read about Lilienthal's fatal mishap and about his gliding experiments. Relying on his findings, as well as on their own, they devised controls aimed at preventing accidents of the sort that killed Lilienthal. In 1903 they became the first humans to fly under power—a great step made possible by the trials and errors of themselves and others. The Wright brothers' experiments were not without mishap, either. Orville Wright broke a leg and four ribs in a 1908 crash of his airplane.

WRONG-WAY RUN

Early in a 1964 football game between the Minnesota Vikings and the San Francisco Forty-niners, a San Francisco pass was completed, then fumbled. The ball bounced free. Players of both teams tried to grab it. Then Viking defensive lineman Jim Marshall scooped it up and ran sixty-six yards to the end zone. The trouble was, he had run the wrong way. Instead of scoring six points for the Vikings, Marshall had scored two points (a safety) for the Forty-niners. As it turned out, the error was not costly since the Vikings won the game. But Marshall was mortified.

The kind of all-out, quick-acting play that led Marshall to run in the wrong direction—once—made him an outstanding player in scores of games over a span of more than fifteen years. It is that record, not his wrong-way run, that is fondly remembered by Marshall's former teammates and by football fans.

HAPPY ACCIDENTS

There are sometimes surprisingly good results when human plans go awry. These happy accidents are called serendipity. By definition, serendipity is the achieving of good results without seeking them, as a result of accidents or general exploring or pioneering behavior. The key requirement is that the good result is something unexpected. A failed experiment can have a good result, and so can the failure of a person —like Columbus—to find what he or she seeks.

Some important discoveries have been made as a result of serendipity. These include X rays, radioactivity, and a chance discovery by the French chemist Louis Pasteur in the late nineteenth century. To study chicken cholera, Pasteur was raising in his laboratory the bacteria that causes this disease. His work was interrupted for several weeks, and unknown to him, some of the bacterial cultures weakened during his absence. When chickens were later inoculated with these cultures, they failed to develop the disease. A fresh, powerful culture of the same kind of bacteria was then inoculated into the same chickens. To everyone's surprise, the chickens still did not get cholera.

Some people might have dismissed this as a puzzling, failed experiment. But Pasteur, who once said "chance favors only the prepared mind," realized that the weak bacterial culture had given the chickens protection against cholera. Within four years, Pasteur had developed such weakened cultures, called vaccines, for protection against not only chicken cholera, but against anthrax and rabies as well.

AH HA!

TO ERR IS STILL HUMAN

For every happy accident there are millions of schemes that just go awry, sometimes with bad results. There are false starts and dead ends galore. It can be discouraging, as dozens of little errors and occasional big ones occur each day.

Still, we have come a long way since the times of Pliny the Elder. We need to know much more about ourselves and the universe, but at least we now understand better how to go about learning. Some individuals and institutions still say, "Don't ask," but many people continue to question. As the noted author T. H. White wrote, these people try to "learn why the world wags and what wags it."

In the process of using our imagination and intelligence, we make mistakes. We can learn from our errors and those of others. We can avoid making or repeating some. And we can also be more accepting of our mistakes as signs that we are human and alive in a challenging, complex world.

Index